T0273194

Reading Gary Lemons's *The Hunger Sutras*, you will enter a dizzyingly visionary headspace, and you will feel your skull crack, ear imp, spirit throb. Expect to be transported at vertiginous speed to an apocalyptic postmodern world where "naked angels / [Lie] in the sand like industrial debris" (re-see: the paintings of Bosch and Bruegel the Elder), this wondrous topsy-turvy, twisted, gnarled-up world (O Revelation) where "melodious ashes fill the air," this "compost pile" realm of the tail-flailing snake, Lemon's own re-invention of the Damaballah of Haitian vodun but with a Buddhist twist. Be convulsed, be transmogrified by snake's prophecies, by snake's obfuscations, by snake's teasing secrets—O, indeed, allow yourself to be enraptured by snake's riddling words, by snake's shape shifting thoughts, this animal shaman "befriender of the dead," this trickster that dwells in the here and the there—omniscient as an "atom in an eye," this roving seer that seeks after truths (the many, never the few) and like some avenging angel "detonates all the lies she's ever / Been told."

—Orlando Ricardo Menes

In this, "the book of last moments," I find myself healed from deep sorrow. Living at a time of private and global crisis, it is difficult to believe in the value poetry. What good is a book in a world without a future? In *Snake: The Hunger Sutras*, I was able to shed skin and become vulnerable—I was given time and space to feel again. As I followed Snake through her/his epic journey (a serpentine movement between life and death) I was reminded of "why I love to die." In bravely facing death, Snake (and the reader) is able to love again. As Snake puts it, "This is me in your mouth—you in mine— / Let's stop chewing—before we disappear." This is the book I've hungered for my whole life; it is the book of our times. It offers us what few words can—an undeniable sense of hope.

—Nicelle Davis

Snake:
The Hunger Sutras

BOOK III
of
Snake Quartet

Gary Lemons

RED HEN PRESS | PASADENA, CA

Book layout by Ann Basu

Library of Congress Cataloging-in-Publication Data

Names: Lemons, Gary, author.
Title: The hunger sutras : poems / Gary Lemons.
Description: First edition. | Pasadena, CA : Red Hen Press, [2019] | Series:
  Snake quartet ; book 3
Identifiers: LCCN 2018036847 (print) | LCCN 2018038618 (ebook) | ISBN
  9781597096898 (e-book) | ISBN 159709689X (e-book) | ISBN 9781597096874
  (tradepaper) | ISBN 1597096873 (tradepaper)
Classification: LCC PS3612.E475 (ebook) | LCC PS3612.E475 A6 2019 (print) |
  DDC 811/.6—dc23
LC record available at https://lccn.loc.gov/2018036847

The National Endowment for the Arts, the Los Angeles County Arts Commission, the
Ahmanson Foundation, the Dwight Stuart Youth Fund, the Max Factor Family Foundation,
the Pasadena Tournament of Roses Foundation, the Pasadena Arts & Culture Commission
and the City of Pasadena Cultural Affairs Division, the City of Los Angeles Department of
Cultural Affairs, the Audrey & Sydney Irmas Charitable Foundation, the Kinder Morgan
Foundation, the Meta & George Rosenberg Foundation, the Allergan Foundation, and the
Riordan Foundation partially support Red Hen Press.

   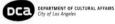

First Edition
Published by Red Hen Press
www.redhen.org

Acknowledgments

The poems "Flat Earth," "The Biter Bit," and "The Big Empty" first appeared in the *Notre Dame Review* Issue No. 45 in 2018.

Love and Gratitude To My Parents
And Teachers—Visible As Well As Invisible—

In Particular

Nöle Giulini

Dirk Nelson

Erich Schiffmann

Anne Jablonski

Norman Dubie

Carie Garret

Jenny Van West

Clint Willis

Sam Hamill

John Huey

W. Nick Hill

Hanno Giulini

Xulia Duran-Rodríquez

Kelly Lee

Anette Berg

Christine Schmücker

I am also deeply grateful to Red Hen Press and their amazing staff for the support and trust I've received over the years, especially the invaluable counsel and contributions made to this book by Kate Gale, Mark Cull, Tobi Harper, Keaton Maddox, and most particularly Deirdre Collins, Rebeccah Sanhueza, and Natasha McClellan, without whose editorial gifts and creative insights this book might have remained unfinished.

This book
is dedicated with love and gratitude
to my best friend and beloved teacher and soul diva
Nöle Giulini—

CONTENTS

Chorus

Chorus

Chorus

Chorus

Chorus

Chorus

Snake:

The Hunger Sutras

Kantakoope Ksut Pipaasaa Nivrttih

—*Pada Three Sutra Thirty-One*
The Yoga Sutras of Patanjali

Chorus

The straw men suck bones from the soup
Where nations boil—their breath like pink spume
Above beached whales who come ashore
To pull these men back to the sea—

The men of straw suck bones through the tiny
Pipes of vestigial hearts—decanting rhetoric
Like wrecking balls swung into clock towers—

Into mud chapels—into nurseries—girders—
Schoolyards and gods—into themselves—
Into bottles labeled with the names of things—

The straw men love a glittering now—
These men get drunk by chugging
Tears squeezed from battle flags (like skeletons
Pulled from old shipwrecks)—so drunk
They unzip purple flowers with their tongues—

They may drink hemlock and detonate—
But only into a larger denomination
Of a standard backed by gold.

There is only one pulse in the veins
On the wrists on the arms of plutocrats
With unlit cigars dangling from chapped
Lips at the wheel of a locomotive that is
Off the rails and running on fallen bodies
Lined head to toe between variations
Of ignorance generously described

In print as conflicting strategies about
Partitioning what light remains—

The straw men gather around the wheel—
None of them care to steer but all of them
Want to pull the whistle and as one hand
They do—wooooooooooo—wooooooooooo—

Heard downwind near the petroglyphs
In a crumbling canyon by the last coyote—
Who licks his penis—then licks the eldest member
Of the commune in the canyon wall.

Fire touches peeling bark which accelerates
The stage fright in a piñon grove—just
Enough for the trees to imagine naked angels
Lying in the sand like industrial debris—
Depleted—toxic—unsalvageable—Delilah
With sand-filled eyes and scissors—

Chasing a red-faced braggart
Using his tiny hands as a megaphone to auction
Flowers to impoverished bees—

The chorus has no choice—snake
Didn't ask for a witness composed of the dried
Glue fallen from the joinery of things
That are gone—she didn't ask for a watchdog
Barking in the backyard of forever—
With moonlight sloshing in an empty bowl—

A bush militia pushes a pilgrim
Out of the wheat directly into the path
Of the next verse where so much attention
Mills true believers into dinner rolls—

Into this—or that—or a hammer
Digging a grave for a nail—

The pilgrim wears a bib and has
A nutcracker in one pocket—a revolution
In the other—what happens next is personal
And resolved in the dark—

Or this child with a gun spitting
Apple seeds at a grateful bird—rat-tat-tat—

This tablet—etched by peeled sticks—warning
Descendants not to eat a purple root—

The pilgrim is years into solitude like
Giraffes on a waterless plain with necks
Long enough to sip from mountain lakes—

The pilgrim is anyone escaping everyone—
Who seethes with lust for the mermaids in a tear—
Where the text of an aquatic principle
Drips sweat inspired by painful shoes—

Down there—the aquifer remembers
The iron taste of cannonballs—the crusader's

Armor dissolving into threads of sodden
Togas perfumed by oil of Gilead—

Once you have eaten the spermaceti
From whale foreheads—used by legionnaires
As a styptic for deep gladius cuts—once
You have illuminated a dark path with
Candles made from the wax of whales—
You will find yourself among flowers sharing
A conscience with scissors—

The frozen twigs in the winter orchard
Feel the dead peel them with stiff fingers—
Sending a yeasty mineral secular longing
For Shakespeare through the heartwood
Until these expressions of comedy
And tragedy produce mouthwatering fruit.

Even the rain lets up enough
For a flame to flare in the blackened
Hills momentarily eliciting the faces
Of animals and children like a hand
Offered so quickly by the time you reach
For it it's gone—doves perhaps—
Rescuing sunrise from a fingernail—

The journey leads out of love through
Sorrow then back into love by way
Of growing luxuriant hair on a bald
Pate just before the limo hits the tree—

Wind fills the sails of fighting ships
As easily as it sinks the captain's launch
Bringing mutineers to judgment—

It sends one spark across thousands
Of acres of dry grass to reignite
The wooden spoon of a chef—oh yes—
We are never so far apart that even a poor sestina
Can't break down the wall between us—
This is a journey back into story
Which appears in the mouth only to be spit out
Like Odysseus coughing blood on the black
Ship among his frozen crew—

Smelling the decayed intent of the cruel
Words before they flow over the world
Like spirits trapped in waterfalls—before
They become cudgels to reduce songs
To whimpers—then silences—or at the very least—
Swallowing the syllables used to encourage
Children to inhabit old mirrors.

At the end of any age—say—this
Age of innocence—it's too late to put back
Everything that escaped the inattention
Of the dream police—too late to cast spells
To grow limbs from bandaged stumps—
Too late for Humpty Dumpty or
To piece back together students
Scraped from hobnail boots—too late

To squeeze nonfiction into the tube
Used for brushing a president's teeth.

The crock pot is plugged
Into a national treasury where
A stew of slaughtered shadows
Are cooked long enough to make
Into wigs for ghosts—or politicians—or—
Whatever frightens everyone—

Here the sun is stored in escrow
So other realities—improbable as it seems—
Can borrow against the dimming light—

The stew is cooking into a paste
Or perhaps a gravy filled with smiles
And grimaces and winks and throats
Spitting out the same chicken bone—there're
Blood sausages—mild coagulants—there's
Bone marrow and hair and this feast is often

Presented to the accompaniment
Of a slobbered horn—

Think not on the shrill music
Or the ambulance running away
From the city toward a full moon
With a swan inside—

Think on the conductor above the fire
Inviting the orchestra to stand while
Melodious ashes fill the air—

Snake's a déjà vu machine—
She lives everything again
And again—each time discovering new
Abracadabras in the compost pile—

She lives outside the implications—the
Fragments—the voices—the promised
Music of a quarter turning to the chatter
Of teeth in a bag—she finds the lost
Mantras from silent tongues becoming

Water running through backyards
And bridges and slash piles—over
The graves of animals through shelters
Slack with bodies slumped in Sterno fumes—
Running through the empty world—through the
Flooded fields to meet the rising sea.

ONE WITH EVERYTHING

Snake looks around the planet
After the original contraction—when
Earth rolled everything into one bite that
Snake swallowed first—felt her tummy
Writhing with parasitic voices—
The coagulated dreams of wren
And prophets and ox—the burnt
Feathers of emu—the sly tick of cat
Feet on nightingale floors—

She hears the temple bells struck by
Medieval peasants long after
The temple was torn down for
Firewood—these things and the clatter
Of palms in hurricanes—the tidal
Swell pulling crabs apart
For gourmands of the littoral
To reassemble with beaks—there—near
The heart—the child picking
Glass from the carcass of a dog
After the smart bombs came—

Snake is a bucket with a pilgrim
Inside—lifted out of a well dug
Directly into the chest of a nation
Infected by a granulated faith
That rocks the cradle with a sword—

She's a traveler with no canteen
Approaching a hill where sheep

Lay like numbers from a discredited
Theorem in gorse thick as spittle
On the lips of a priest waking
From teaching Latin to demons—

Snake climbs that hill—everything is
Gone except the ghosts who
Creep up on the sheep with shears
To make coats to ward off the cold
Rain that keeps the dead shifting
In their holes with the anticipation
Of rising into a stem—into

A flower—where willingness
To forgive the living intensifies
The color of the bloom.

QUESTIONS OF TRAVEL

Snake remembers the storm
Outside her little house—the wind
Like a flail with a silver tip
Whipping a vampire's back—rain
A sideways river and the night
Blacker than the devil's grin—

Remembers her favorite chair—
With a wool blanket over her
Feet—chamomile tea steaming
In reach—small light
Flickering from a sconce and the
Narrow beam of the reading
Lamp illuminating the collected
Poems of Elizabeth Bishop—

The storm swirls around the windows—
Looking in—snacking on fears
Rising from the trees—eating the small
Lights as they push through glass
And are absorbed—snake turns
A page—reads *Questions of Travel*
"And have we room for one more folded sunset,"
While the bare lilacs beat the window
With tiny fists of new growth—

She sighs—comfort—everything
Just right—spine straight—the lamp glow—
A woman's voice—the wool blanket—

The comfortable old chair and the smell
Of tea somewhere between cut hay
And essential oils on a razor strop—

Then the lights go out—the storm
Comes inside—it's dark—so dark nothing
Is visible—there's no direction—no up or down
Or sideways—just liquid darkness ruling
The kingdom of the momentary heart—

She hears children outside
The window—looking in at her—saying—
"I see a ghost."

The poems stay—even after Elizabeth
Fell through a trapdoor into another house—
After the book is burned or banned or simply
Aged into a papery tomb—the poems
Stay—read to the past while the future shatters
Windows looking for someone to blame—

When the book ends and travel is
Over—we—the poems—remain.

SNAKE PATROL

Be a long time coming—
Billions of years roll by
And nothing moves under the sky
But snake's rippling foil—

She misses dogwood—white and shrill
As dawn's first light—misses hollyhock
Climbing a weathered shed to declare—
In honeyed shrieks—its stigmatic
Adoration of the sun—

She hears the dead sift like coarse
Flour through mesh into delicate powders
Maniacs snort before telling stories
That are probably true—

Snake wanders the increasingly
Empty landscape of thought—listens
To everyone that isn't there—

The dead are her constant friends—
They expect little more from her than cotton
Lavender offers the Shroud of Turin.

The dead love snake—she carries
Their dreams to high places where they lie
Like camellia blossoms on stony
Slopes—where the past provides topsoil
For hope to flower inside of hearts—

Where each cup of memory—steeped
In loss and cooled by breath—tastes
Of the screams beneath the avalanche.

THE LOCKER

So many things never said to anyone
But myself thinks snake—

So many concerns left unspoken—feelings
With no air slowly suffocating in distant
Chambers of the heart—carried like cyanide
In a tooth waiting for the time suicide
Is preferable to a stranger's touch—

Snake decides to let them out—
These prisoners of a mind grown silent—
So pressed between choices
They dried into an adder's tongue—

Only there's no one left to hear
Snake finally proclaim his long stifled
Joy and gratitude from the bottom
Of a well dug deep in a mirage of pain—

There's nothing left to listen.
And it listens.

Water

Snake likes to take historical figures—
Real or imagined—don't matter to snake—
And bathe them in the common tub—then
Bottle that water for the marketplace.

Oh snake be one of the world's first reptile
Kings—sellin what's left in the bar rag at closin
Time to the first customer of the new day.

Snake remembers Earth one time
Dropped a stone that rocked the world—
Floodin everything—giant waves
Tearin down mountains—crashin
Through windows—makin bridges
Into barrier reefs—rain like woodpeckers
Chasin a feller with a wooden leg—

Everything drownin—swallerin
Spray—dentition in the muddy flow—
Earth—workin herself free like
A cat so obsessed with cleanliness
It licks its nasty tail completely off—

People done forgot that flood—worry now
Bout heat and smoke—worry about
Fire—cause most days they drink
Accelerants then light a match—

Snake knows fire is a flood in disguise—
Got hydroelectric dams in pristine wilderness

Torturin rivers to send hot currents back to
Houses so as to overcook a critter pie—

Fire and water—two heads—one
Hat—either plenty sufficient to
Address the current infestation.

LEADERSHIP

There's an orange-haired puppet
Sitting in the front row of snake's disbelief
With its hand inside its pants and the fixed
Look of a musketeer with wet powder
Fleeing across a bloodstained field
From a recording of its father's voice—

Snake sees old prayers caught
In spiderwebs—still juicy with hope—
Hung for next year's child to eat—

But what if there is no next year—
What if this must be addressed—right now—

Snake never underestimates the attention
Span of maggots—who—though slow as a growing
Tusk—manage to reduce the questions
To the scream elected criminals illicit
From justice with gavels made of flesh—

The scream is the music of our times—
Which are gone—and were never ours.

THE BIG EMPTY

Snake was there when
The world was consumed—

She was an atom in an eye
Watching Boethius in prison swallowing insects
That swarmed between his gangrenous
Ears like a dark and mobile ring around
A distant planet politicians are excited
To announce is suitable for primitive
Life forms that function best in the dark.

Boethius—held for three weeks
In a baptistery surrounded
By marble walls smeared with holy
Water and the excrement of bats—

Then exiled to wild country
Near a forest where he watched
Through curtained windows ragamuffin
Children take home green branches
Used to whip their legs—

Like all deep thinkers he was
Bald at an early age and plucked
His eyebrows and sometimes
His genitals and was inordinately
Proud of his muscular calves—

None of this saved him nor
Consoled him when the rough cord

Was pulled so tight his eyes
Popped to the floor and watched
Prayers drip from his mouth—

Snake hopes Boethius listened
As well as instructed the invisible woman
That remained in his cell throughout
The long silences before death—

It's no one's fault that—in the end—
The blind cartographers—who in summary—
Are all of us—wave their empty plates
At the conjurers lurking off the trail—
Who have a history of shouting clear
Directions until the pilgrim's weary foot
Touches the cloth across the covered pit—

The important moment at death is not
When the breath ends but just after—
When the wax of the afterlife forms into
The candle the next one born will light.

I—Snake

I—snake—don't agree with the laboratory
Ghouls who wear white coats like
Brides while tormenting the eyes
Of rabbits—there's blood in the corner
Of a moustache—pressed from a smile—where
Part of a shark wants out—

On the floor near a hosed-out cage
A small furry thing with four legs
Tries to swim in the eddy near a drain—

I—snake—am sick of it—the eye droppers
Filled with answers—the tiny head
On the master of ceremonies telling
Everyone the main event is a trapeze act
Where acrobats believe the net is real—

Let's just get it over with.
Let's volunteer to confess something important
To the dead that will anger the living
Enough to make them stop
Opening and closing their mouths
While sitting in the corner with a pointed hat
Taking turns eating a fly—

Where the sun touches down
The horizon is a streak of red—like the feather
In the hat of an Oscar Wilde impersonator—

Or an apple tree under a full moon
Surrounded by new buildings—

I—snake—see parents dandling
Skeletons—see white bears dancing
On a pinhead of ice—see skulls
Where an ocean lost its mind—see whales
Swimming home to the sky—as if evolution
Is a matter of staying one step
Ahead of the murder of habitat.

Which I—snake—say—it is.

ISLANDS

The ghost clicks the stem of a dead
Pipe against its front teeth while contemplating
The soldier about to fire a first kind word
Into a defenseless enemy who is prepared
For amputation and death but not
For generosity—the ghost remembers
How god-like it was to live—how coming
Out of one dream into another is
Like a blind man in a banquet hall
Fingering a passage from plate to plate—oh—

The ghost listens to the monologue
Of the voice rumbling down the corridor
Of snake's throat like office furniture
Moved rapidly from place to place
In a sublet apartment above an old
War veteran living on a pension
Insufficient to keep her crushed leg
From seeping into the sheets.

This voice belongs to all of us—
Or really—the river belongs to the sea—

The ghost falls backward—
Making a snow angel—into the years
Death took from it—falling back to a time when
Father left Butch Wax on pillows and mother
Listened in on party lines—when only the heat rising
From the slow decay of love kept the clenched hand
From aiming pistols at flowers—

On any given morning we might
Awaken from this dream—lying beside
The beloved in time to see everything recede so
Quickly it's gone before we know
It was never here—just a momentary
Swan given shape by the hydraulic
Pressure of innocence holding back
The charge between two shields—

There is no map for anyone—no blueprint
Assigned at birth that shows how to build
The edifice in such a way that it will remain
After the ground cracks open—no way
To take off the gloves while pulling triggers—

Though all the lost wanderers who gather
Inside this bipedal ruin agree—everything
In the mirror must soon be surrendered.

The End of Pain

Snake pulls a bullet from her heart—
Studies it—holds it to the moonlight
Falling on the country where she spends nights
Stacking stones around herself to keep
A private darkness penned inside—

Like a broken wisdom tooth
Coming through the gums years
After extraction—these are the bullets
Hard times shot into snake that only come
Out in therapy sessions where the forest
Confesses it loves fire more than rain—

When she lives inside a single
Point of light—when the cry of a naked child
Across still water turns to ripples
That come ashore as fully clothed adults—
The healing of the visible begins—

This bullet looks like a face
Once entrusted to care for her—
That instead blew childhood into a balloon
Floating among roses and thorns—

Over time the injuries—the hard
Hands—purchased joys—this frozen
Stream beneath which one fish drowns
In a shrinking bubble of air—provide context
For the memory of sleeping nude in a room
Where moonlight on a toy soldier is the only warmth
Left for the world to take away—

Only those soldiers—only this body—
Only that world—moving in all directions home—
Hoping the reward for vigilance will
Melt the frozen lines between nations—
Between siblings—between the voice calling for
Its lost shadow running through the night
From the rising sun—and that other voice—
Describing a reservoir filled from below—

So far away you may think you
Are called to answer but it doesn't
Matter—nothing will survive
Your silence.

Ballroom Surgery

Colors of sunset are as beautiful
As the colors of sunrise thinks snake—
Going up—coming down—

End and beginning—mortal
Implacable forever packed in-between like
Germs in a thrift shop shoe—

I like you for being who you
Are—says snake to her shadow—there'll
Never be nothing like you nowhere again—
As they dance into the dimming light
Of another retractable goodbye—

Only to find—like an anesthetized
Patient slowly awakening to the surgeon's face—
The operation is still in progress.

BEFORE SLEEP COMES

Snake sees the partial child frozen
In the field—its small hands turned
Up at the wrist—fingers full of snow like
Early tulips—sees hungry wolves—scant
In their rafts of skin—pulled by the oars
In thin hips—under moonlight—shadows—
Dark purple and fast—crossing open space
Between the house and barn—

Corsairs of winter—intoxicated
By the fluttering of black violins that
Professors of bite marks on a bone understand
To be the lullaby sung by moonlight
Entering the temple of a frozen bird—

Snake goes back into the darkness
To help the farmer bury what remains—

Bringing a gun with two bullets—
For the three wolves.

Morning

Snake was angry
'Bout what happened to people
And animals and plants got pulled
Apart in the last rage like a wandrin
Amorini crushin sweat bees
With its thumbs.

She'd think about them politicos—
Got a glass of hemlock in one hand—
Other hand on the button sittin
Round in some oval office smirkin
At the stink on their hands
While burpin up entire populations
They done swallered like some
Hillbilly can't keep from drinkin
Out of the toilet bowl—

But no more—anger in snake
Flooded dry riverbeds—boiled memories
Of beauty and joy and cut new gouges
In old muscles—causin bones to
Break and fluids to fail and ideas to
Pop out of the air already armed with
Weapons of mass conviction—

She don't want to turn
Into the thing she's fightin against—
Don't want to let da resistor—brah—
Become da capacitor dat be suckin all dat juice
Out of de light fore da circuit
Shorts its own damn self out—

So snake rolled that anger
Into tenderness squeezed from the cells
That dream of it—took little bites—oh
It was tasty—like licking an envelope
With a love letter inside—

All the hospitals disappeared—
No one disturbed the orange parakeet
Learning to curse the media by imitating
The talking heads buried to the neck
At low tide—there were other consolations but
Now only this huge hole in the heavens
With a ghost—yes—in midair—

Not falling—not moving in any
Direction—mumbling nonsense
Astride a heavy machine—
Before the drone acquires it.

Unanswerable

What be an ocean?
What be a vein?
What be a corpse inside a body?
What about old whale—propeller
Cut in both eyes—struggling
Through an acid tide?

What crawls through numb
Tissue like infantry into countries
Oppressed by leaders so ravenous
For power that soldiers and civilians
Drink visions from each other's eye?

Who bolts out the gate
With a grimace—favoring an old wound—
Never finishes the race—believes
Endings are mythical?

Who never plays with others?
Who is self-confident as a clean
Spittoon near a dirty well?

Who lines up scarecrows
Against adobe walls and shoots
Them with crows?
Who grinds hospital beds
Into powder to fuel
The radiation machine
Plugged into the spectacle
Called sunset?

An artist stalks the beach
Collecting sand—sifting
Bones and shells and live
Pieces of crab and human remains—
Squeezing this onto palettes—
Painting grim coagulations
Of blue-faced shamans in cradles—

Why do de birds sing
When de sky be so toxic
De rain kill de forest
So dey gots no place to land?

Snake hides among yellow faces looking
Out yellow eyes from a field of daffodils—

Watching the yellow sun go down on
The corpse—chasing a phantom leg—
That won't stop walking away.

LANGUAGE

Snake outlives her deaths—
One at a time she sheds them
Like woolen scarves that make
Her cleavage itch—in a myopic darkness she
Removes her spectacles—then stumbles
Into someone milking a cow—

Like a fox deep in a winter
Hole under falling blue snow dreaming
Of clucking hens—snake
Awakens to the crash of desires
At the crossroad of hunger and shame—

She hears—through the snow—
The bombinations of dead monks
In abandoned calcium emerging
From the movement of a tanager—
She hears laurel sigh—knows—if she stops—
She'll wake up as stone.

There's also a howl coming
From the lips of an old man chasing
A packrat—that stole his wedding ring—
Through burned slash near a frozen
Creek—this memory is no more
Than yesterday assaulted by vegetables
Scraped with the sharp edge of right now—

Snake thinks these thoughts
In the traditional way—carries

Them in her head like a bucket
Of water between two fires—

She don't launch them as missiles—
Shoot them at strangers—she
Don't build edifices out of love
That topple from the imprecision
Of an engineered regret—

She chisels thought slowly—
With great tenderness—from an ancient
Wall of primitive noise—precursor
Vowels piled one growl at a time
Atop the beginning of language—the guttural
Inference—grunted equations—torn sinew—
The taste of things alive—

Even when the choir stops singing—
Enough music remains in the wax of the ear
To build a scented candle by whose sputtering
Light it's possible to read the epilogue

That explains—hunger is no friend to truth
But plucks the eyebrows of its absence—

A hermit wobbles on crutches
Toward a cave where a greasy ochre
Radiance puffs out of the crude paintings
Of bison speared by horsemen
On a smoke darkened wall—mercy flows

Into those who run from the dazzling
Dentures of the crowd that is a smile
In the same way promises are weapons.

We see it when waking up to a hard
Rain—sleeping naked in a fast river—see
The water part around rocks that glaciers
Placed—exactly there—for us to understand—

Those who cherish the world—and they are
Among us—may be us—are notable not just
For the quiet sunrise in their touch—
But for the safe house of silence they offer
To the victims of the spoken word.

MUSIC OF HANDLES

This is a pilgrimage—
Snake's in pursuit of her tail—
Which flails in a universe
So far from any current reality
It might belong to an alien body—
But no—it lives in the same
Mirror as her face—both moons
Locked in declining orbits—

Like all of us she's enamored
With the possibility of a mythical journey
To a joyous place where self-discovery
Is a thriving roadside attraction
On a gleaming one-lane blacktop between
Abandoned places in the heart—

She gets out her telescope
To survey the night sky for the light
She may have left behind—

There's little evidence in nature that
Wholeness exists except for sunset illuminating
Prayer flags torn apart by wind—

The mountain trembles from the jocularity
Coming from the dark mouth in the rock—
Where a coven of giggling mystics paint the walls
With images of their goddess flitting through the jungle
With the tool civilization needs to survive—

Or perhaps it's not a mountain
But a historical marker dedicated to the last
Politician who refused a bribe—

Snake sets the book of last moments
In a bucket of tears—the ink mapping
The roads to paradise turn the water light violet—
The color of pansies crushed beneath
The pink hooves of piglets in the rain—

The lines blur into one another as borders
Do when those on either side shake hands—

There is a wanderer who studied
This book before visiting every village
To tell children never ride on the backs of wolves
Down a slow river if—on opposite banks—
Adults shout different truths at you—

Overhead the sun is momentarily
Blotted out by something shot down
For describing this—as if any graphic
Account can offer safe landing to an epitaph—

To see one another dissolved by joy—
To see the darkness in each other die—
To grow old beside another growing old
And not look away when both faces fill
With so much love they recall the genuine
Light on the long muscles of a dream—

Is to drink the violet ink in the bucket
And spit out unwanted personalities—

Is to remove splinters from the foot
Of a creature running away—to fry regrets
Like crepes in the thick oil of sorrow—to burn candles
In a paper asylum—yes—yes—we have loved
Each other enough to desist swallowing
Shadows at the end—to say it—together—

This is me in your mouth—you in mine—
Let's stop chewing—before we disappear.

EN PASSANT

The eye of god opens—sees
Snake—closes—snake's still there—
God thinking—snake's sneaky—
No matter how bad the lighting—
That cat be everywhere.

Snake wants to live at the edge
Of town in the back of a sheet metal
Bar where ragged men grind stained
Molars all night with jaws big as engine
Blocks—where her sisters dance
On tables in the scarlet strobe from a broken
Sign with rooters in each hand.

She wants the door to open—
Speckled light pour in like tongues
Into a jigger glass—remind everyone night's over—
Outside possibilities are appearing
Like beards on a corpse.

Snake wants things like they were—
We all want things like they were—
And because of this—they are.

COURTSHIP

The frogs pull snake out of his jalopy
Then tongue lash her to the bumper
As they frisk her tail for contraband truths
She might smuggle into poems.

Like most of us snake lives inside a parcel—
On the stoop of an empty house—freshly
Delivered from another planet—

Consciousness runs through culture as well
As through body—the way rain in a forest
Drips down from branches and is absorbed
By trees who participate in self awareness
By learning to drink with their feet—knowing this—snake
Takes a chance—detonates all the lies she's ever
Been told—or told—at the border—where they attempt
To enter the promises exchanged between lovers
Addicted to the worse attributes of one another—

The rain keeps on falling—the wet parrots fly
To other climates to get dry—snake stays where
She is—recognizable only to herself in the rippling
Puddle where new offerings of love—made without regard
To gender—inhabit the old nativity.

Last Supper

Snake floats in beginner's mind
Where hope and its zygote—
Fear—tremble with the understanding
Tomorrow is another day at
The all-you-can-eat buffet—

She knows hunger glues things
Together like drunk drivers and pedestrians
On wet roads—where the language
Of skid marks is something like the
Benediction from a stone axe—

She acknowledges the ghost at the wheel
Reeks of kidney pie—sees tractors without
Drivers tearing apart black earth
Beneath which spirits writhe
In cut pieces that regenerate when
Snow covers the field.

Snake goes to the rocks—says—
How you do this—sit around maybe
Millions of years like me and don't
Eat nothing—rocks say—*we*
Moe'uhane dat ono tween meals brah—

Bumbye we geeve 'um bruddah—
We like no grind da kine brah—

This does nothing for the pi dog
Biting its tail in the gray
Morning within range of the rocks thrown
By skeletal boys eating lesions from
Their father's beds—somehow
The sun rises anyway.

It's nothing but crooked syllables—
Crunched around a couple vowels—animal
Sounds between the jaw and tongue—
Like honeybees in a lion's head—

These words—at the last supper—
Gratitude filtered through something
In pain—becoming—amen.

Chorus

It steps down from its saddle—
Lays a rough hand on her shoulder—
She sees cataracts cover its eyes—there's a galaxy
Smudged by faces wanting out—
So benevolent they burn
Like stars in the hour before dawn.

It says—come snake—you need help—
You're not alive or dead—you think
Breathing is what it's all about—so
You need to die. Here

Is your heart—see how shriveled—
Like a fetish some warrior
Hung in the sun to remember—you
Surrendered—see—your heart is empty—
Good—now you can begin.

Empty it of emptiness.

ENCRYPTED

Snake gathers the dust
And pours it in her ears—she
Hears it—packs it in her eyes—sees
It—until the songs that lie dormant
Like groans beneath a battlefield
Become intelligible story—

There's the squeal of wooden
Wheels hooped with bronze
Turning a corner in the arena
As men in leather tunics stick tridents
In each other—horses maddened
By tigers—blood on the sundials
Where daylight drinks with birds—

The miniature in the exhumed locket
Shows a round-faced vizier—in a brassier—
Accepting a nostrum made of rouge
Scraped from the inside of a veil
By a man in a blue suit with orange hair
Slicked into a pompadour by blood—

Snake can't look away—can't—nay—
Won't—plug her ears to the soundtrack
Featuring the music of nocturnal
Emissions gurgling in the historical
Bowl every narrator sips as a prelude
To the oral tradition.

Eventually the concert ends—

A man speaks from a funeral
Urn so softly it's as if he's talking from the pages
Of a faded journal—saying—

"Put me back in my La-Z-Boy
With the sports channel on—
Shower me with gold like King Tut—
(buried with a donkey—he's my favorite honky)
Beer in one hand—remote in the other—to the applause
Of corkscrew and noble pork rind—"

Around this voice—same as always—
The story glows like atmosphere
Sticking to a burning rock in space—

Then a woman whispers like wind
Blowing across a hidden microphone—
Or is she singing—perhaps she's the wife
Of this man—just offstage—a song
About the punishment for those who try to
Force their way beneath her dress—
Snake watches her take the urn
From the mantle and smash it—

At this point snake understands
Why the butcher shop draws the shades
When hanging the freshly slaughtered goat
Before the morning crowds stroll by—

The woman sucks the ashes into a vacuum—
Puts the bag back on the mantle—

As if
An understanding between
Thirst and rain is possible—

Though once in a while
She drinks the melted ice from the drip
Of frozen dreams and opens her
Cold lips to spit out the bones.

EARLY TIMES

When snake was a fish
She got hooked then tore free—

When snake was a wolf he got his paw
Trapped but chewed it off—

When snake was a bug she got
Crop dusted and evolved—

When snake was a whale he
Got infected by harpoons—

When snake was human he
Was safe except from preconception.

This leads to ponderatin
The final days when the politicians
Crushed the world to powder
And snorted it to improve the size
Of their networks—each one
Thinkin they be a hardass—got a
Regular Blarney Stone lodged
Out of sight in their drawers—

Be expectin the world to line
Up and kiss it for good luck—

Snake curls on a hot rock
But she ain't about to kiss
Nothin be mustifyin in the dark—

Rather she enjoys bein
The only bullet in the kingdom
Of the disassembled gun.

STRUCK BY TIME

Summer is over—

The voluminous cloak slides down
Snake's shoulders into the fallen
Grape leaves—the leaves that turned
Brown and sound like random gunshots
When she walks on them—

The vineyard as one mind has trouble
Convincing the individual plants that
Only a gospel song in the mouth
Of a buried bluesman keeps
The roots alive all winter—

The cloak is blue—the color of the sky
When no one looks—this is the cloak she dropped
When just a young girl—running away
From parents toward animals that raised
Her with love underground—

The blue is the color of the ocean reflected
In the white face of a marionette partially
Covered by sand on a beach where
It bowled with coconuts—before

Beachcombers broke their legs for fires
And collage artists took their eyes—

Snake disappears into the blue
Cape—the blue ocean—into the brown

Crackling leaves of grape—sinking—into
This earth—toward everything waiting
For the mailbox to speak in tongues—

The transfusion between this moment
And the next takes place like twins
Exchanging confidences about their therapists
While driving an ambulance toward a collision
Where the Jaws of Life are used to pull innocence
Out of cruelty and shock it back to life—

The medics know where to stop because of
The flares on the highway that warn them
A life is dead ahead.

CHRISTENING

Snake got euthanized by degrees—
By lies sanctified into truths chasing
Ordinary life into shadows while exultations
To the gods call down tons of heraldic light
That—once it landed—emulsified inside
Reverence like bones in a broth—

There was the sense the plumbing
Failed and lavatories returned coded
Messages from the lips of a guest baptized
Downstream of a corporate takeover—

Prejudice wandered the potential
For violence in a guitar string—whew—
The plumbers were up to their necks
In the unpleasant music made when
Profit tunes its voice to the sound
Of flies beneath a shroud.

One day she enters a remembered forest—
Sees distant flickering light where broken
Angels—like passengers from a downed jet—lay
With manikins in the glow of money burning.

The recovery happens then—
Even as the injury occurs—this beginning
Of a true understanding about what it means—
Not just to be alive but accountable
For the unlikely gift of the next breath—

Prepared—without immunity—exposed to
Every blessing and disease—to relearn that
The valves of the tangible never close.

LOCAL WOLVES

For Abner and Harper and Sophia

Snake sees humanity rising in lockstep
Toward figments in the sky—toward a
Brightening cloud while around them shadows
Sip the view from graveyard eyes—

The local wolves are hungry
For any song that opens with a bass note
That's rhythmic and not built upon
The thumping of a withered fist—

They wander the upper reaches
Of the lightning-struck tree—nesting
Among bare branches with the winter
Birds—whose realistic philosophies don't
Include a place too cold or dark
To sing—together they compose elegies
Honoring how storms in one mind
Strike lightning in another—may become
Two hands flying without bodies
Toward a blue note—or burn the unsigned documents
Declaring a state of war exists between
Falling snow and the gesture of a mime—

Snake forgot to mention that
Ice sticks to the fur of the wolves—shivering
Like prehistoric shadows left in the glacier
After the animal moved on to play
Accordion in fields of summer wheat—

The now-empty branches
Click together with the quiet
Desperation of broken hymens
In the ears of palace guards outside
The room where Caligula
Lavishes an old vowel into the paragraph
Of a ransomed daughter that mingles
With her fear into the historical
Description of sobs trapped in a pillow—

The secret cure for longevity
Is as simple as a rockslide above
A ragged hermit bent in prayer—

Breakthroughs don't happen in a vacuum—
They occur when deadly obsessions
Push citizens from windows in towers
Behind a burning veil.

WHO? ME?

I—thinks snake—I—
What's that all about—where
Did I come from?

Oh yeah—this rank old
Pastry got something sweet in the center—
Tastes like chocolate but just
Might be the forehead of a baby mouse—
Better ask da cat bout dat reference—

Eat it anyway—sweet—
Tangy—bitter—playful—joyful—
Filled with love or dog-faced
Among foxes in a hole—take a bite
Old snake—then watch how
That *we* gets filtered out of the *I*—

Into the cosmic perspective—
That calls itself the posse but
Has no badge and rides alone.

FLAT EARTH

Snake thought the earth
Was flat in that she believed
Every side of anything is always the same—
One country—one person—
One mountain—one tree—
All the same country—person—
Mountain—tree. Even when roosters
Tear up ribbons behind the red
Vials of medicinal holly snake keeps walking
Toward the vanishing point knowing
When you jump from a high place
The world starts over where you land—

In the same way neutrinos
Supply the gravitational scaffolding for galaxies
To fool physicists into believing there's
Enough light in the universe for everyone
To be seen—snake understands the fundamental
Signature of all life—the avoidance of pain—
Offers a topology by which a big wave
Surfer predicts the conditional grace
Required for the perfect ride by measuring
The volume of her mother's tears—

Traveling in one mind will
Do this—make you crazier than a hawk
Pecked by doves—the seemingly infinite
Roads of forever—caught in one
Dimension between the toes—
Give the weary pilgrim false ideas
About the complexities of shoes—

The path leads to an origami sunrise—
The simple folded into the beautiful—
No more to be worshipped
Or fought for than territorial water
In the eyes of the drowned.

The Biter Bit

The table is set—groaning
With thymus glands and hummingbird
Butter and sardine paste—all
The wonderful engulfments
The mouth can barely keep
From eating when they lived
Much less when properly cooked
On fine china by candlelight with
Biber's Passacaglia in the background—

One who is so corpulent
He's admired for the sheer
Yardage of his well-cut bib
And the entire animal it took to make
Her purse—taps a knife—shining
With tallow—against a crystal goblet
To momentarily diminish the gusto
Of the eaters as they gobble
The faces lost for all time—

Slicing the centuries with boning
Knives into manageable days and hours—
Before stuffing them into cavernous
Mouths designed not only to savor
Worlds—but crush them as they do.
When he has the attention
Of the gathered gourmands she
Stops tapping the goblet—
Proposes a toast to the success
Of a life so well conceived
It results in present company—

They get down to the heavy
Succulations—while snake—in the kitchen—
Prepares a jellied quail by defecating
A small dream in the aspic—

A dream of velvet antlers—
Of fur—of roots—alive in a wilderness
Of plates—running from forks
And knives descending like hail on a glass
Coffin—the sacred dream songs
Of Jonah—dissolving into the silence
Of siblings pierced by harpoons.

INQUIRY

Snake does her best to describe
The mirage perfectly—every detail—
But the closer she gets the more confusing
The input—like a cauliflower ear—
How does it taste and what does it hear?

The descriptions fail—she needs more
Words to say exactly what is true
And what looks out at truth
Watching the audience
Through holes in the safety net—

Closer still—and the mirage
Puffs out more bright smoke—
More evidence it's real—yikes—snake
Sees hog lots and choirs and sea foam—
Something wiped on an envelope—sees
Clowns in suits with tiny hands balancing
A nation while lowering the toilet seat—
Hears frogs composing literary criticisms
In puddles left by heavy trucks—she
Sees children behind old faces
Smoking like tires in snow—

The dead appear—many familiar—
Some family—all part of a strategy
To enforce the fiction of a borderline—then
Scarecrows limping past assembled crows
Who—like the lunatic—believe in the restorative
Powers of summaries—who offer this
If asked—*caw*—and—yes—*caw*—

There's bunch grass in the hand of a nude
Woman dancing on a prairie just before
A tornado mixes the wildflowers at her feet
Into sachets hung around the chins of
Men on horseback whose spears bleed
The colors of the setting sun—

Remember—to the men—the woman
Is also something to be speared—

There are antlers on the head of the muse—
A child finding its fingers in the crimson
Folds of its mother—new information
Bowing pizzicato on an instrument
That shoots bullets when strings break—

Then snake steps right into the mirage—
And finds it empty—the music no more
Than the conductor gasping because the
Horn section took carminatives—

Nothing here is real—nothing is true—
Not even the perversion of love disguised as need
Naked in the green room with appetite.

Snake wanders through lives in the dark—
At home inside the glow of truth that calls
Her toward a greater distance—and with complete
Devotion—and little regret—she follows
The firefly off the cliff.

Chorus

Free—
Of conveyors toting bales
Of tissue closer to a fork—

Free—
Of the gun barrel making
Conjugal visits in the thicket
Of a toothy smile—

Free—
Of razors poised above wrists—
Slicing the sunset deep enough to color
Flocks of crimson doves
Circling the formation of sorrow
Inside the bone palace of a primal
Urge—where original uncertainties
Drip from a potable howl—

Free—
Of bankers paying strangers
To bark—yes—free of the medieval
Fluency of the garrulous
Friar extracting faith with fire—

There's nothing left to devour—
The eaten resurrect in the precious
Gestures of a Loblolly pine asking the dead
If it's enough to share the rain—

It's a time free of catching
Diseases simply by looking
Too long at angry faces—free
As this wet dream trapped in
A folded sheet—flirting with
Oblivion in front of a mirror like grandma
And grandpa in their underwear—

Free—
To lick the tears that drip
Like icicles hanging from the dereliction
Of imaginary youth—not caring
The dark perspective drinks
From the same broken prism as
The victims of a personal light—

We bloom and fade and bloom
Again on both sides of the breath—
Something in a cradle floats across the lake
Of the long pause among reflections of
Things to come—when it's time
Everything stops moving except what
Just happened swims away.

Quantum Loop World

Don't look away don't look away don't look away

The voice inside snake's head won't
Stop no matter how much thinking
Gets piled around it—saying things
Like—relax—let it unfold—or don't
Get in the way of the river—or—hey
Snake—no matter where you go—
There you are—or snake's least favorite—
Dude—chill—the sun's on its way
No matter your dark bereavements.

Look away look away look away

Then one morning the sun
Didn't come up—for anyone anywhere—
Except snake—fragments of gardens
Where truth hid underground all winter
While mirrors popped on frozen vines.

Don't look away don't look away don't look away

Then the feeling of relief—of peace
Snuck through the snake like smoke
Signals from ancient fires—so dispersed
By time and wind no message remains.
Only the charred ring where the lessons
Were eaten but remain unlearned—

Don't look away—look away—don't look away

HUNGER SUTRAS

In the garden of mirrors snake swallows
Fragments of her tongue—the wind not enough
To explain the litter of broken souls
Or the torn blossoms scattered in the dirt
Near each last breath like hot ingots burning
Through falling snow beside a glowing forge—

What is a body if not a fragment
From a larger body—the husk alone—
Afraid of the perennial candle
Whose light can't warm the basement of the heart.

Still—snake don't like most of this pedestal
Marmalade folks be spreadin all over
Legendary critters chillin critters—
Be sweatin—gruntin and deliverin
Stone killers up the spine into the eyes—
Wipin away each tear with bloody hands—

She comforts each piece as it forms over
Again and again inside electric
Bundles of meat—behind fences of skin—
On farms where faith and tissue lie trapped
In pails of frozen moonlight until night
Subsides and the heat of the coming day
Maroons the sleepers inside a darkness
Without borders—where a gently offered
Touch is all that's needed to tenderize
One shattered drop of light into a child—

There are scriptures struggling to describe
The miracle of life to the distant
Sun receding from view as it colors
The sky the pigment of an open vein—

Abandoned—left to chance—the body dragged
Through conflicting choices where a halo
Of smoke from roasting flesh adorns the blue
Mouth of the sky eating the mountain top—

Snake feels insights gurgling in her guts
Like bad mouse—rancid frog—or bitter dreams—
She understands nothing dies except old
Stories—which never lived except inside
Desires energized by action verbs—

And if a sudden lock of hair falls past
Your eyes—something unplanned like that—then dear—
See the shadows stop running from the sun—
See how life becomes visible again—

So much depends on the positioning
Of croquet wickets in soft summer rain.

The summary of everything that's gone
Can be seen in the movement of a broke
Down creature stumbling between two dark
Shelters protecting a burning candle
From the enormous presumptions of wind.

Sometimes the tribe murmurs gratefully while
Roasting a harmless plover over flames
As the gods of thunder swallow its screams—

Sometimes the night is just the night with no
Subdivisions other than the phantoms
Reciting homilies above a grave.

Shattered fingers reach from an avalanche—
Reach for stars—the night—falling snow—sending
Cries for help to anything that listens—

Winter is the marketplace where magic
Is sold to pay back rent on promises—
Some lives are trapped in terrible climates—
Like old growth trees ensnared by toxic clouds—

Or silver hair gleaming in red rock cliffs
Above blown carcasses in bad water.

This is a war in which lives slam into
Lives like dirty towels inside the minds
Of abbots responsible for choosing
A modest color of black for young nuns.

It is the aftermath of bells ringing—
Of incantations lost inside severed
Tongues—when the mystical force of the earth
Surges upward from its heart into spring
Flowers—somewhere in a cradle the soft

Propulsion out of an infinite light
Turns into the narrow view of right now—

Children know the path that cuts truth in half
Can only be erased by walking it.

Walk the corridors in the mind of snake—
Avoiding ancestral ghosts like hobos
Stepping over crossties on railroad tracks—
Here the dead negotiate their losses
Into a single proffered rose the wind
Tears apart—then reassembles into
A black bird nesting atop a lightning
Struck steeple—singing melodious songs
It learned in the still egg of forever.

There's fables glowing inside dark weather—
A storm or flood—rising inside the coils
Of snake—that is just a boot coming down
Hard on a crawling bone—there's tomorrow
Pinning shadows against the charged night air
Until babies wake up inside of them—

Wake up to a world rejecting the one
They came from—a place where bodhisattvas
Roll ecstatic masters in the falling
Snow—whispering—if you believe nothing—
Then every moment is a miracle—

When we live at the expense of others—
When our survival is joined at the mouth—
Even our most cherished lies grow black fruit
That's leavened with misery into song—

Karmic smells bust from the guts of the world—
Revealing more than the thermometer
In a roasting hen—or the sharp edges
Of the imaginable—throwing chips
Of restraint from the spindle of a bride
Dragging her husband's beard through the fire—
There are spectacles hidden in ditches
Beside the narrow road—if you wear them
It's possible to see invisible
Gods spurring lame horses into a trot.

Soldiers in direct light hate their shadow—
It has no eyes and is too hard to kill—
Prefer instead the taste of old brandy—
Sipped directly from the mouth of a gun—
Before rearranging the citizens
On the patio furniture so crows
Can fly away with their evening meal—

In summary—everything is just born
This instant—even the one-armed bugler
Playing taps above an upturned cradle.

The zookeeper so to speak never sleeps—
Because of this no one is permitted
Out of their cage unless accompanied
By a muscular angel who patrols
The darkness wearing nothing but a thong.

When the eyes open to the first moment
Of the returning—there will be visions—

Something like a mastodon or redwood
Or wolverine or a field of bluebells—

Ladled out of tears then distributed
Between molecules like a liquid arch
Joining mountains to the colors of dawn.

We flash like fire in a drop of dew—
We feel the architecture collapsing—
Leaving the roof of the flower standing—
Beneath which—while the shovel sleeps—a wax
And hooded figure in a flaming cage
Writhes to the applause of its enemy—

Or perhaps a sudden flare in the mind—
To chase flies from the carcass of the truth.

All of this is kept hidden from the lost
Tribe of explorers asleep in windows.

Billions of years of gods' blood on snake's tongue—
She sleeps inside her dark oven as life
Cooks at the edge of her snore—dripping raw
Sunlight—exuding stink—becoming tree
Or bird—sliding into a living cell
Like a queen sneaking up on drunk servants
Fondling one another on her throne.

In this first instant—when the DJs mix
Flatulent angels with kerosene breath—
An unwritten story begins to write
Itself with ink supplied by a bitten
Tongue—the story goes like this—mortal fear
Of being swallowed alive—whether by
Family—friends—or forces of nature—
Inserts into marriage the subtle taste
Of copper pennies in a magpie's beak—

Out of the conflict to live or die—
Comes snake—the anvil—snake—the hammer—snake—
The crushed violet exuding its scent
In metal-lined rooms of yellowing fat.

Other than regrets from a life misspent
Collecting and mounting phantoms nesting
In crevices under the skirts of hymns—

Snake is pleased to awaken as root wad
Beneath a carnivorous red flower—

Her journey is a dance through dark tunnels
Toward bonfires inside a buried mind—

Sees her fellow pilgrims sleep—the endless
Souls flitting in ambulatory rags—
Here the faces of oracular swans
Emit botanical screams as they land
With decreased vigor in a tablespoon.

It is the suffering of the unnamed
And forgotten that turns the desert sky
Purple—gathering the final victims
Of impoverished gods in the vulture's
Beak—who devours them in an empty
Nest at the top of a falling tree.

The underbrush is surprisingly thin
Where the light's blocked out—the gray trunks of trees—
Knotted as the veins on the swollen legs
Of old soldiers on porch swings—high above
This story—drip from invisible leaves—
Monkey urine—resins—a corrosive
Rain from the nocturnal lust of orchids
For the host that must die for them to bloom—
Dark as the wet spot on headrests where

Elderly couples dream of their lost love.
The machete rusts away in the hand
That broke when adrenalized by a rage
That grew wings to carry the wanderer
Over a battlefield where surgeons treat
The gangrenous wounds of standard-bearers
By taking out the organ that forgives.

What's savage about any land transfers
To the occupants waiting for sunrise—
Where meadows transition into forest
Or shiny stones become a killing axe—

What is always beautiful is secured
Inside the petals of a winter rose—

Or etched in mud by the traffic of storks
Beside a river filled with drowned cattle—
Or the vagrant red centipedes—seething
From partially buried skulls that still plot
Strategies of war inside steel helmets—
Under these splinters of a broken cross
The soldiers are making peace with flowers.

Snake remembers shadows in the triage
Tents sharing ditch water from a small canteen—
Sun resting on waves no less perfectly

Than on the faces of axe-scarred warriors
Hunting the banks of a bloody river
For children holding hands underwater.

In every case the ghost of what is said
Is haunted by the things it didn't say.

In snake the jiggle of mixed corpuscles—
Like matadors dazzled by their own capes—
Erupts in a catastrophic shimmer
That needs release—that wants to begin—
But must wait for the terms of surrender
Only this heartbroken earth can reveal:

Article number one—   no explosions—
Article number two—   no measurements—
Article number three—   there is no small—
Article number four—   there is no big—
Article number five—   this is your home—
Article number six—   practice your song—
Article number seven— look at it—
Article number eight— love what you are—
Article number nine—   dance with the wind—
Article number ten—   death is a dream—

Sweat sponged by the bar rags of history
Drips on the empty pages—the parched lips
Of the drunk men touch the shot glass—the tears

Of cold crows—the loud pop from the boneless
Sockets of branches when the monkey pulls
Out the white grubs of its future to eat
Them alive because only on this path—
Sustenance given by death—can the night
Protect the orphans listening in locked
Rooms to blaring trumpets—the thud of flesh
On flesh—the sound of the sword going in—
The music of phantoms waking up born.

Then silence—as the first garden party
Ends when the ribs are taken off the grill.

When the carnival departs—the trees grow
Quickly over its absence and the king
Of seeing nothing but what isn't there
Is restored—things ignite when they forget
They're everywhere—no authorial rain—
Or cup of tears—can put out this fire.

The horse collapses under the rider
Who forces it past every waterhole
In an effort to outrun the sunset
Before it amplifies the emptiness
Of this journey toward oblivion—

Like the turtle carried aloft by gulls—
That drop it from great heights on the rocks just
To taste the meat of sorrow in its eyes—

It's the interior language of crows
Filtered through a propeller spun by wind
That enflames the external marketplace—
Where a wagon bouncing down the highway
With the heads of goats hanging by their horns
Announces to the village that dinner
Is arrived and will be served by fallen
Angels freshly squeezed from disappointment—

No one will ever ride this horse again—
It will be impossible to forget
That it died drinking from the empty page.

Our meanderings are no different
Than savage currents undermining trees
Along the steep banks of flooded rivers—

No different than schizophrenics making
Bricks from paternal voices in their heads
Suggesting the mind place its derrière
Against the window to the outside world—

Soon I will stumble away from the tramps
Who salute me with glasses full of drool—
I will tremble one more time in your arms—
My poorly designed but beautifully
Rendered—easily admired—sadly
Coveted—quickly lost—world without end—

I loosen my belt—then pull down my pants—
Urinate behind the bar while patrons
Applaud from the shaded doorway because
They understand—without these sensible
Precautions I'm likely to pee my pants—
A thing I've worked a lifetime to avoid.

My friends—co-conspirators—my licking
Cats and salivating dogs that always

Bark at the strangers I don't see until
Intimacy overtakes me—thank you—
For your gifts—your consummate blah blah blah—
For your love—and the way you provide one
More breath just when it's needed to compel
The stationary blades of the windmill
To spin fast enough to pump the haunted
Years from the remains of an injured child.

Tonight the windmill fills the trough with blood
Reflecting back the rising harvest moon—

The scarecrows straggle from the harrowed fields—
Pull the sticks from their ass—then brush away
The dead insects before bending to drink.

Intermission

The earth is accelerating gently—
Snake hears the lyrics of the past chanting—
Like mystics caught beneath an avalanche—
"Oh how silently the dinner bell rings"—

This and the accumulate weight of snow
Falling on soldiers humped around a king
Who walks graveyards wrapped in his country's flag—

Attended by shadows—that—like captured
Crickets in gold cages—cry for the sun—

Since this is an intermission serving
As both prelude and epilogue please note
The witnesses—the underbrush dwellers—
Evolved from anteaters—who must decide
What lives or dies inside a rotten log—

Earth feels the heavy footprints sinking in—
The drill bit bite—the sucking pipe—the trash
Percolating toward her core bringing small
Flecks of inconsolable—demented
Dreams—feels increasing pressure on her spine—
Memories of sunrise—of broken hearts—
The last synapse of something in the mouth—
Thoughts blown out the nose—new images
Re-painting the wallpaper of right now
The color of a rabbit in the snow
Thumping out the soft music of goodbye—

It is impossible to imagine—
Though demonstrably true—that birds grow wings
So they can fly into a shotgun blast.

How the sky continues out into space
Without borders other than where the dark
And light swap an ephemeral French kiss—
The way aristocrats and babies suck
Equally hard on the same thumb—how all
The bipedal curiosities—brought
Forth from entangled particles of greed—
Build sand castles along estuaries
Where misguided emperors encounter
The beaks of revolutionary gulls—

There's no time for the pedantic speeches
Of smart bombs—or the blasphemous whispers
Of swords or holier-than-thou spew
Of professorial insecticides—
Not sacred instances conferred by priests
Or the brass shavings from a warrior's eye—

Only a willingness to use brushes
Dipped in sunset can paint the morning glow
On the enameled faces of the dead.

It is finally apparent that we
Are immigrants on both sides of the grave—
Even the shroud—even the clothes closet—
Seems like a concrete bunker between two
Countries at war—blowing up the other's
Land with different calibers of angel.

The struggle to contribute anything
Of even minute value requires
Complete attention to the feather broom
Propped in the dirty corner of this dream—
Snake knows what might be true—she built her house
On the solid rock of what isn't there—
Assuring that the future will provide
Mystics and architects with the same job.

On the border between the forceful touch
And the galvanic ripple of damaged
Skin—something resembling a small boy
Finds a suit worn by the man he'll become
Lying in the mud beside a mangrove
Swamp—where the knobs of exposed roots glisten
Like the bald heads of enchanted elders
Buried to the neck as the tide comes in—

Oh—it's not a boy—once the waves pull back
We see a ravenous monkey eating
Crabs from the suit's lapel—searching pockets
For instructions on how to stop hanging

From its tail—maybe it's looking for coins—
Or zippers to pull down high in the trees—

After deciding the suit doesn't fit
The strange animal returns to the beads
Of sugar on the stamens of orchids—

Everyone in this story—which is true—
Is assured another generation
Of beasts will suffer the arbitrary
Glance that turns living creatures into food—

The steam coming off the teakettle left
Too long on the stove is merely the breath
Of petulant gods with an erotic
Obsession for the last of anything.

Symmetry underscores the songs of clams
Opening to let the moon inside long
Enough to harden cold light into pearls—

In snake there's nothing left to hide other
Than her reflections in funhouse mirrors
That summarize the theological
Doctrine of worms inside a casket flag—

Snake was there when the world ended—she saw
The good Samaritan burn the house down—
The towers spouting meat smoke like fathers
With mouths stuffed with menthol and cigarettes
Repeating the lessons baptized in lies.

Snake lives on the border between things—feet
In the desert—head in the jungle—mind
Inside the crotch of the suit of the man
Undulating between mangrove roots like
A cataract shifting across the eyes
Of gods worshipped for extracting revenge
On those who think enough is not enough.

Consider there are two brothers—or two
Sisters—or two monsters in a story
About monsters counting rosary beads
In the dark beneath the bed of a child—

Twins from all physical appearances—
Both transparently animated states
Of disorder magnetically captured
By grace in the same way cruelty is drawn
By stars from graves to offer back as light—

It is the same with loss and abundance—
With anesthetic and operation—
With release and grip—it's like this with roots
In high wind—with doubt and trust—derision
And faith—it's like this inside and outside—
Wherever something is—its opposite
Waits with a long reach, a bib and a fork.

To be tied to a bench in the middle
Of a revolution is a sure way
To end up as fog on a windowpane.

Only then do the generals advance
Toward the fences around their property—
To see the fields are planted with local
Conscripts—and—when the poppies turn scarlet—
To bottle the odor of rotting flags.

We live because we eat one another—
Tear down to produce the stool we sit on—
And live on—even in death—given new
Shape in the dark—built by cosmic forces—
Taken back apart—put back together—
Always whole—though never believing this—

Snake holds tomorrow by the ears over
The flames as it burns away excess fat
And writhes in the greasy light with the cold
Grace and blank stare of an elderly mime.

It's the honorarium of evil
To lease bone scaffolds along the borders
Where the shy alluvial light gives birth
To evening and its orphaned shadows—
Leaving behind the unanswered questions
Crawling into each other in a failed
Attempt to repair what isn't broken—

Snake watches her body with interest
As it swells then pushes out a life form
With the trembling vigor of hangmen
Placing a rope around an outlaw's neck
While drinking whiskey with the other hand—

In snake, creatures are flying between trees—
One—bolder than the rest—drops down to feed—
Lands on the hot animal between holes—
Then eats the answer in its bulging eyes—
Paint this with rifle fire at sunrise—

There's a window with a view that changes
As faces move past it like a light show
Reflecting on the gold fillings in smiles
Unearthed by fire ants—that sleep inside
The palace of ideas where hunger turns
To worship—once a sufficiently bright
Light shines out of instinct—it's possible
To feel mercy and tenderness spinning

In the slow centrifuge of appetite—
This worship is only winter building
Snow angels in the furnace of a rose.

What can be forgiven is forgiven—
The sutra is not to *live*—but to *be*—

Choices—the genie escapes the *carne*
Asada steaming between the ribs
In each living lamp—the genie is free
Now—to write equations on the blackboard
The solitary mind mistakes as truth—

We hear the words unspoken at the end
Of life when prayer replaces medicine—
The children at lonely intersections
Watching their parents build statues of gods
That future generations will tear down—
It is possible to sleep forever?
It is possible to awaken now?

Blue heron—leaving peace signs in the mud
Where it wanders—questions—how to fly—
Not just away—but into what comes next—

In back alley dumpsters—in marriage beds—
From vascular light spreading on the floor
Beneath parishioners touched by Jesus—
From the hollow staff of a nation's flag—

Whispering rivers as silence rejects
The urge to shout humbug at nurseries
Filled with new ears becoming microphones—

It echoes between the gun and the sky—
Sings in the soft barrel of a slapped child—
Lives in the red drool from a broken vow—

Flies over the struggle—lands when movements
End and the bodies settle into earth—
Refreshing the nectar that nothing drinks
Without losing everything it believed
To be real—even the lips of angels—
Dripping with doubt—might spit curses at god
Or sing praises to the revolution
That begins and ends with the human heart—

This is the garden under falling snow
Covering every scar made by the hoe—
This is the flower we never planted
Growing from the body we couldn't save.

SNAKE'S FIRST PIE

People came late to the party—
Before them—the world's pretty much
In balance—plants—animals—workin out
Agreements allowin for grace within
The clench of the prime directive.

Snake remembers creation myths
Mostly have different sized wheels on
The same wagon—fibrillatin bout
Emptiness swirled into existence
By a fatherly hand placin
Objects in time to scare the locals
Into the abjection called worship—

Don't really matter which story
Describes the recipe—all got
A pinch of guilt—a cup of blood—
Very little remorse and a recyclin
Plant at the end of the road.

Nothing changes the story—
Except when the victims tell it.

PROMISE

Snake's tired of being the bad guy—
Pointin out the brown oblong
On the dinner plate or remindin folks
That closin your eyes just means
Things might be creepin closer.

Snake didn't start out like this—
She loved the smell of horses
On a brush and striped light
Through the hackberry leaves—loved
The weathervane spinnin in circles—
And cottonwood plumes twirlin in
The air above larks drinkin
From a small freshet—

She loved everything
There was to love about livin—he
Did too—snake didn't want to
Drag the darkness behind her
Like a brother with a runny nose.

She ain't no vampire suckin blood
From historical events cause she likes
The taste of sufferin—just don't want
The forsaken left behind.
Look here—can't help but see
It happen—seventeen billion passenger
pigeons—folks thought they'd never
Disappear—see em everywhere—one flock
Took fourteen hours to cross the sky—

Whole trains got rented—fat cats
In Pullmans leanin out windows
With shotguns blastin the little doves
From trees—where they be restin near the tracks—
While porters run beside the cars like gun
Dogs—cuttin the breast out—leave the
Wings still flappin in the dirt.

Not one of them birds left anymore—
People too busy with a knife
And fork to look up and see the bloody,
Ghastly truth of what's gone.

Snake knows how it feels to recede
While being dragged into view—she
Knows about the beautiful tiles handmade
By local potters caked with blood
On the museum floor—

She understands what Schopenhauer
Meant saying something bout how all things
Be distressin upon reflection—

There's no other way home it seems—
Except through these locked doors leading
Into the infinitely precious—unfortunately
Delicious—temples of the other.

Chorus

The last riff of the sax melts out of the
Refrigerator like spring snowmen built
Hastily by children grown so old they
Don't believe in magic hats—

Father—we have lived without you
So long the rifle in the corner has become
A slender birch in the wallpaper mother
Used to cover the hole in her heart.

From world we come, freshly dead,
New to spirit, fumbling without shape
Inside stillness profound as a small
Fire burning on a frozen lake
Thousands of miles from the window
Where children dream a golden moon
Will light their lives forever—

Light eats fire to shine. Shadows
Eat the night to hide—in the middle—
The fence is strung with gestating
Platitudes that don't understand one
Reality slams into another—until
The pieces are beat so small it can
Be verified that everything is here—
But only right now.
If snake was anything but snake—
If you or I were different in any way—if
We'd taken the blue pill—not the red—or dropped
The ball when it was thrown—or forgiven

Ourselves in time before the peripatetic axe
Cut scarlet flowers from dead trees—

If the nurses who smothered
The last parent in the purple fog
To the sound of ventilators shutting down—
Were actual angels—not patterns cut by pinking shears—
Everything would—still—be—the same.

Inside the ambulance at midnight
Medics struggle to save the patient by
Injecting the siren with silence.

Snail's Pace

Snake thinks about thick syrup
Waking in the roots of a cold tree . . .

Jingle of bells, creak of wagons—
The toppling round barrels as the wheels
Hit ruts made last year—horses'
Ears pointing forward—swish of tail
So much like falling snow snake
Shivers in her limbic glue—

Later the sap boils in great chrome
Vats until the songs of the forest
Live in bottles like imaginary friends
In a child's lost hat—

These memories come at snake at
The speed of light—so many they're
Forgotten as they happen—

They keep on anyway—rippling
In all directions like an hour
In a pool of years—though it's possible—
If snake dives deeper into silence—to find
Them again—like old friends who once
Shared an umbrella in the rain.
At the end of the day—the forest
Is empty—the sadness of the leaves
Transfers down to the ground which bubbles
Up in rivers where animals take
A morning sip from another world—

Elsewhere the table is cleared—
The candles snuffed out—
The room darkens—and not even
The rattle of bone china disturbs
The dreams of the headwaiter.

INTENTION

Snake hides in the trees beside
The road while big trucks speed by
Like sculptures fired from the minds
Of artists at the air.

Snake times the right moment to send
Her shadow across to the other side—bam—
Shadow gets run over—rippling
Awhile—then dead on the road.

Snake tries this again in her own
Body—slithers across—makes it safely
To the other side—looks back—thinks—
There's always another shadow—

Snake disappears into a new world.
Shadow gets up—moves away—
Thinks—there's always another snake.

INTONATION

It's said the bats
In the Tower of Babel spoke
Eloquent Aramaic between
Themselves and terrified
The populace by hovering
Above the ziggurat defecating
Wheelbarrows of fertilizer used to grow
The toxic grains milled into bread
Served to non-believers—

Snake speaks all
Tongues fluently—each
Language dripping from
The forks of her tongue
Like honey from the thumbnail
Of an advisor stung
To death removing a queen.

There's no one left to hear
Snake describe in high Latin the torment
Of Saint Anthony—how he was
Pulled apart in every
Direction—how—assailed by
Personal demons—he gazed
At the face of God with eyes
Benevolent and empty
As tablespoons—how he gargled
Air like a singing bowl—

Or the details supplied by Carlota
Snake passes on in gutter Polish
Regarding the execution of Maximilian—
Whose body was found stuck to the bristle
At the end of painter's brush—
Dry as an old scalp—among muskets
In a secret room in the armory
Behind a cracked adobe wall—

The body that native artists
Love to depict with a red bandanna
In both epaulets—drug through the streets by loyalists
By order of the next tyrant—poor
Maximillan—rolled in honey
Like a pharaoh then sprinkled with gravel—
A food for thought or birds.

Benito Juárez did not see snake
In his boot with a clothespin on her nose
As he watched the smoke from bullets curl
Into a Modigliani-shaped cloud out of which doves flew
Like somber gray chords—mused out loud that

The gun is the only wind instrument
Appropriate for summoning the clergy
From their mattress underground—

Benito touches the window
All the while propitiated
By a serving boy—suddenly the trumpets

Announce the execution is over—the Zapotecs
Running for the jungle—their disordered
Voices escaping the wallpaper
Like blood through heavy bandages.

Snake speaks
These things to herself—
Over and over—inventing
A language that describes
Landing places to a bird—or

This swelling of thought—
Like a bucket of seawater
Hot suns turn to salt—

Snake pulls the ragged histories
Into moonlight where it's determined
They are why the wheel stopped turning—
She washes the chariot until it shines—
Washes the spear points until they gleam—
Patches the holes in the monastery wall
Before sponging the bleat of lambs from the air.

BONSAI

There is an ancient highway
Through the forest that warriors once used
To ascend upon their enemies—stealin, murderin,
Enslavin, guttin, bleedin, skinnin—returnin
With the raw opium of war—

Some things never change—thinks snake—
Except maybe the roads are a little better—
Puttin the ragtop down on her Humvee
On the way to the next battlefield smokin
And bangin at the edge of the horizon
Like sheet metal horses yankin tin apples
From a cast iron tree.

The dead like to joke about
How God is not smart enough to
See that killin worshippers is a strategy
Resultin in diminishin returns—
Nor do they care that at night
Humble dandelions press reverent faces
Against the window but are refused—

Same every time thinks
Snake—the livin sit beside the dyin
Sayin prayers—please let the war
End in our favor—the sufferin stop—
Against the entrance but are refused—

Please allow this patient to live—
This nation to prevail—this faith to rule—because

We alone have the sacred right to impose a
Momentary shape on the wild pine.

MEDITATION

Sometimes snake just wants to
Melt away from her body—like an icicle
Losing its grip on a sunny bridge—
Be boneless—drip—drip—him
And her together in a pool of skin—

Melt through each other's organs—into
Thoughts and dreams and the wanderlust
Inside each cell—further into the silence
Struggling around the tumult of words
Like ravens who gave up trying
To escape a deep and narrow well—

She doesn't need to do more than
Visit the wounds of the harried waitress—
Or the jockey mixing dope in a stall—
Or the banker preening in a polished shoe—
To see there's nothing inside injury but vagrant bliss
Wandering dark alleys—eating from dumpsters
Overflowing with raw desire—bridal wreaths—
A soldier's last letter—onions and blood—

And the bones of Icarus—struggling upward
Toward the dimming light.

A Room with a View

The fierce gaze of the stone
Statue belongs to snake—belongs
To the world inside of snake—belongs
To everything that looks without
Blinking out at a crumbling view—

The gaze was there before
The sculptor found it—inside
The stone—or tree—the unformed—
There's a contagion manufacturing
Appearances mistaken for the truth
That spreads mouth to mouth to mouth—
This sickness doesn't need to swaddle
Revelation in blue ribbons
Or decorous colors to soothe the mind
Or blind the spirit to its bones—
It only needs to be believed—

Snake lives in her head billions
Of years—she understands the world
Is a rented room—owned by a landlord
Who takes scoops of flesh in trade—

Hungry ghosts command the vehicle—snake
Collects tokens while an ephemeral comfort
Steers the passengers over the cliff.

Wormhole

If all things are actually one thing
In infinite disarray—if there's no separation
Between the hunter and the hunted—
If there's such a thing as higher power
From which every design flows—(one is
Reminded at this point of a septic tank)—then
Everything born out of and dying into
The same ancestor must—on some level—
Understand it eats itself—

The spirituality of hunger knows no
Contradiction between the lives of the saints
And the required bone in the mouth—
Those molecules on your fork—gadzooks—may
Have once ignited an unlit cigar—

See the hands of Pizarro strangling
Atahualpa with narrow fingers
Smeared with the grease behind his
Ears—as his warriors tighten
The ropes holding down the sacred vicuña
Prior to cutting its throat—not—in this case—for
Libation—but to show the powerlessness
Of the local gods—who care about nothing
Except preening in snowfields—
(it should be pointed out that the vicuña—
unlike the guanaco—is never eaten but revered
For the luxurious abundance of its wool—
Believed—to this day—to be
The offspring of pack ice and the shadows

Of condors circling a pink dawn—a child
Of feathers and altitude and cold eyes
With the minimal heartbeat of a stone)

Gold lives forever—it melts
Through the ages from chalice to spearhead
To a molar in the smile of a minister
Scribbling moralities concocted in the stall
Of an empty barn while simultaneously
Licking the hand writing them down—

The wormhole opens and drags
Us into the past or the future—leaving
The present with the faint drum roll
Of last-minute remorse lingering
In the proboscis of elephants playing taps
Above an elder bristling with spears—

Snake wanders far from home—
Lost in the memory woods—
Floating over torn pastures where
Livestock come home at suppertime
To lick salt from the earth.

Tomorrow the candles burning inside
The pumpkins on the porch will go out—
And those grinning faces will go dark,
And that orange face will stop smiling.

If You See the Buddha

Snake be afraid all the time that
Nobody sees him so he's jumpin
Up and down—wavin his arms—
Here I am—here I am—
But the wheelbarrow don't stop—
Moves right on by—no one pushin it—

Snake be afraid nobody hears her—
So she's all the time shoutin—hurtin
Herself so as to holler louder—
Here I am—here I am—

Snake ain't afraid no more—least
They ain't afraid of being seen or heard—

They just sit wrapped in the
Warm coat of one another—listenin—
Listenin—to the beautiful lies that
Sizzle like mosquitos in a humid night against
A light designed to kill them.

In the Garden

And don't—at personal peril—
Recall the cicadas arming themselves
With inflections borrowed from skewers—
Meaning—a drawer filled with kebabs—
Shouting out the window to cows
Eating grass in a hard rain—

Don't remember the way
A neighbor hung her brassiere
On the line—her face like a rose—seeing
The windows across the street
Lined with fathers teaching
Parrots how to say—"yum"—

Snake remembers—realities spin
Out of each moment in all directions—
Producing music that compels a diver
In the inner ear to belly flop into the shallow blue sea
Beneath the gift of a sad song—

Oh—our songs—each sound—each
Creature—whether mooing—oinking—
Trumpeting or burbling from an oven door—
Each uttered nuance of thought—
Or reflex of bone—contributing
To the warmth of the sun on a vessel
Sailing further from solid ground.

When Prester John promised Queen
Victoria he would find and bring back
The wealth of Shangri-La—
Thousands of young boys entered
The army—after first sneaking into
Their mothers' closets to try on
Beautiful gowns in order to mitigate a future
Where they must impale each other—

Inspired by these militant excretions
Into mystery—the Prussian explorer—
Alexander von Humboldt—lashed
Together—then drove—thirty pack mules
Into a brackish saltwater lagoon
At the mouth of the Oronoco for no other reason
Than to observe whether the man he'd
Become was the same man that taught
Him how to use a chamber pot—

It's said he wore a red silk scarf
Around his unshaven chin—not for elegance—
Though in his immaculate cavalry boots
He looked a fashionable tool—but
To hide the orchids feeding there—

We only have conflicting stories—a guide
Who telegraphed the details to his wife
In São Paulo—and Alexander's journal—

But both agree—with a pocket
Watch in one hand—a calligrapher's

Brush dipped into a weeping sore—
He made delicate strokes on fine linen rag
Depicting electric eels burrowing
Into the ears of the drowning horses—

He advanced the science of suffering
By timing to the exact second
How long it takes piranhas to force
Winter from the white of an eye—

This is the nutshell emptied
Of everything but the nut—perhaps
If seen all at once—like starlings
Suddenly leaving a dead tree—it would appear

As the leisurely arrangement of ink
In a story about nothing at all—

Priscilla von Butterweisen
Finishes the last pickle in the jar—
Fills it with the tiny candiru fish given
By her lover—Alexander—to reduce salinity
In the aquarium of his absence—

She pours the fish in her husband's bath—
Snake was there—swimming among them—
Encouraging them with her silence—

When the husband returned—hot and dirty
From milking an overtly pink shadow—the fish—
Snake refrained—swam directly into his penis—
Thereby igniting the little friar
Inside the hood ornament of a scream—

Not that Priscilla had any claim to moral
High ground—like most resourceful victims—
She turned her suffering into power then used it
In the perfectly timed execution of every rose
In her bloodless garden of revenge—

This is the opercular spine of fate anchored
Against the forceps of detachment—or justice—
Pushing hexagons through a circular conceit.

Prester John gets closer to the strange—
Throws a spear across a boulder-strewn plain
In Abyssinia at a man with dreadlocks
Rising from a frangible crease in the current
Faith with a guitar in his hand—
Though it is still the Victorian Age
In this poem—the years have indeed managed
To continue to this moment like toddlers
Learning not to step on bees—

This is the three bar blues played
On a Stella six string—the music of faith tuned
To love—this is how trees grow tall beneath
A stone bridge—this is why a single tear
Can put out rainforest fires—this is the reason
Strangers often accelerate away from each
Other so fast nothing remains
But the ash at the end of a smile—

In snake's mind the starlings leave
The dead tree all at once—startled by a sudden darkness
Previously believed to summarize the scalp
Beneath an unwashed wig—

Snake wanders the empty planet looking
For the window through which
She can escape the anguished cries
Beneath the broken dam.

Volcano

Snake swallers some backwash
Before addin her discord to the hootenanny
In time to lip-synch the last goodbye—

The songs get more audible and less
Inspirin as golden daylight comin through
The stained glass windows turns into night—
Lyrics driven by grimed pistons bout
Dreams that be real as propane tanks
Blown into silver boutonnières—

She whips the fragments into forward
Movement so it appears there's more than
A cart filled with emptiness pulled by
Sketched horses—the garden
Of self-discovery is experiencing winter—
But don't tell that to the ejaculators
Trapped inside the gravid bloom—

Snake comes to a mountain beneath which
There's a cave where a long time ago
Something happened—

Snake hears the girl's voice—
Even now—as the poem is written—
In the thin air of yesterday—the grunting
Men sealing her inside the cold silence
With her blood on the walls—

The elders go back to the village
Promising the hunting will be better—
And the tribe will have food—

Snake enters the cave—hears
The girl's voice—louder each passing year—
Until the mountain explodes.

Chorus

Frozen hills with clots
Of red asters popping out of snow like tiny
Ghosts hung by shrill songs
From brittle green scaffolds—

The hills live forever but this snow
Fall is new—the remains of wisdom landing
On each generation like dandruff
On the stooped shoulders of a priest—

A seldom seen light in the woods is
Tapped from the glow of soldiers lying atop
One another below a rest area
On a highway that leads between
Variations of nowhere—

Who inside their rotten clothes
Embody the grand design of history that nesting
Birds carry aloft in shreds.

It's all sacred thinks snake—leaving
This offering in the deserted chapel
Beside the ocean—on the way to dig moonlight
From the tide with a broken shovel.

THE AERIAL VIEW

Snake remembers watching
An elected windbag filling a hot air balloon
With all the promises made throughout
Time to all the creatures in need
Of an aphrodisiac for hope—

Balloon puffed up so big it dwarfed
The earth—ghastly old patched thing swollen
And fermenting with undeliverable love
Letters and the bogus machinations
Of a process designed to facilitate
Cross species amnesty at a barbecue—
Like so many words—great to chew
But difficult to swallow—

She was gonna fly away
On that balloon—take an
Intergalactic tour around her tail—
See the scarecrows shoot their cuffs
And dance around the starving crows—

But the weight of sorrow—of unopened gifts—
Kept the whole contraption from rising
Any higher than the bare trees
Above boot hill.

Smoke Signals

Snake remembers the smoke
Coming from the barrel of a gun—
Un-aimed but recently fired—
Gives off the same stink as the wet seegar
In the mouth of the tuba player
Marching in the parade celebratin free
Cocktails at the Epstein bar and grill—
Be takin a hit then puffin
It through the coils of the horn
Like a bullet made from sound
Unsettlin the feathers of a bird-brained crowd.
Feathers of the patriotic crowd giving
Everyone a bad case of rin tin tin tinnitus.

All them what likes to glance
In the hole of something about to erupt
In smoke got a sign etched on their face like peep
Show rubes at a knothole watching
A midget shot from a cannon—smoke
Everywhere—man in the air—
Hot dog on a stick—

This is when—if you look carefully
At the next act waiting behind the dark envelope
Of canvas where human cannonballs
Land—you'll see a head-down elephant—
Ringed by pudgy mahouts with bull hooks—
Hurting it just enough to make it perform
Without making it visibly bleed—

Keeping the audience applauding
While torturing animals in the name of entertainment
Is tricky business—requiring complete
Genuflection to the spasm of green in a wallet
And a willingness to throw sawdust
Over everything that leaks out—

Snake be sick of smoke—sick of talkin
Bout it—seein it drift over cane stubble—
Hearin it comin out of library
Windows where the same alphabet describin
Jesus be burned for followin
Them teachins to a natural conclusion—

Snake remembers it as it ended—
People lightin peace pipes with one match—smoke curlin
Off citizens drippin out of window sills—
Families holding hands while the daily
News shows men with their pants on fire—

It's burned into the mortar holding
The present to the past—the future adrift in mid-air—
The shadow of the dark-eyed bombardier
Moving silently across the land.

Village Smithy

Snake observes Lord Cod study
The oaf shoeing the young stallion—the Lord
Anticipates the kick between the legs
Before it happens—already
Deciding whether to reward such
Carelessness with a few weeks of limited duty
De-lousing blankets or with a shallow
Grave in the forest—where family
Members are permitted to gather
Mushrooms after autumn rain.

It was then the laughter
Of the patriarchal gods—so many
Of them—fell on the barnyard
Like thunder—their beards like old flags
Pulsing with moths—like determination
Beneath a tortoise shell—like
Sabers inside sheaths savoring
The holy tang of war—

The Lord can't afford any more
Unemployed oafs hobbling in plain
Sight between meaningless chores
Just to keep them alive—goes into his drawing room
With a sheaf of paper and plume
And quickly sketches the design
For the piece that still bears
The name of Cod—respected for its
Brief tenure as a root cellar for vegetables
Attempting to stay fresh in the dark.

The smithy receives the hoof—
Damage happens—this time the smith
Is hauled away in a cart for a short recovery—
Before the swelling subsides enough
To sit on a stool inside the barn
Cleaning curry combs as the filtered
Yellow light makes even a purple
Testicle appear sacred.

Snake lets go of every instant—
Knows time heals time by mixing
The permanent with the antidote for death
Called—by some—love—by some—the top floor
Of forever—by others—simply
The mirror where real angels hunt
One another in the twilight hours
Before faith goes blind and the lump
Beneath their wings grows hands.

Snake understands—what comes next—
Though fictional—depends not
On the aggregate darkness under the dowager's
Chin but on the flecks of light fallen
Like sawdust to the floor beneath
The appallingly beautiful prosthesis already
Fitted for the lame years to come.

CATCHING WAVES

Vlad the Impaler enjoys
Pounding tent spikes
In the earth to stake out his maniacal
Attraction to an invisible root—

Like everyone—though—his best
Intentions break free of his moleskin vest
To walk free as a prisoner among
The daughters of his enemies—

His motto is—no one is worth saving
Because everyone is saved—

Snake sees this and whirls
On her tail so fast she momentarily
Completes a circle within which forces
Create a universe with one livable
Planet upon which citizens develop
From one-celled organisms into creatures
That can't refrain from extracting agreements
From each other with pliers.

Snake sings to the fading red feathers
On the old cardinal with the broken
Beak lying still as the snow covers its
Shy dance—sings to the refugees holding
A child above the cold waves as memories
Of warm sunlight on a wooden handle—or a simple
Song sung quietly to early fields of grain—
Are replaced by a tug from below—

Where a scrap of paper fluttering in a school
Fence contained instructions telling families where to
Hide when dragons fall from the sky on
Fire—the ink is faded—the instructions illegible—
The backyards gone—the parents now pilots—
But the children—like penguins—refuse to fly—
Inhabit a new world where it's possible
To give back what was taken in their name.

calivester doshon abotheria
desleeb losidestrell bosus blunerko
saliveredi lindorvon gelthistra llium—

replacendo magainstio prandistum ragainstio
lomystrel ladonely englovello—shamendora

SNAKE FINDS A SKATEBOARD

Snake remembers the time when
The Earth blew its cork—pinching sediment
From its wound—gone completely seismo from the
Bad stink of carbon in the laundry
Chute—smudging things into a red mist that hung
A million years over the frozen oceans until
Earth finally felt safe enough to sleep—
Dreaming of the next you or me or the green
Spindles where fruit hangs—these new
Things that don't quack or drill or spew
Songs of shame back at the silence.

Snake wanders the landscape like a lozenge
Melting under the tongue of someone who
Can't sleep because their throat's on fire
From saying things they don't mean—

She sees a skateboard sticking
Out of the empty river just now exposed
After all the eons by the movement of her
Tail—now snakes don't mind admitting
A billion years or some such number without
Company can drive a person off the road
Into a rest stop filled with ghosts
That jabber in a tongue snake understands
But wishes she didn't because the ghosts
Are repeating the founding documents
That stripped flesh with promises—

Snake's got calluses on the stumps
Where wrists were when she was a boy—
Or a girl—been so long she can't
Remember what she was—which
Brings the revelation that it doesn't matter now
And probably didn't matter then—just
Be someone—as best as you can—

Snake jumps on that skateboard
Like a wooden puppet on a carpenter's back—
Rides it—in balance—pushing faster
With her tail—carving the breezes with her tongue—

Bending corners—jumping rocks—
Getting air—accelerating—wind up her nose—
Heart light as a lullaby—losing her breath
Toward the end of the ride—the
Abyss a sudden dark opening before her—

Snake goes for it—she flies off into
The epic view—mysto in the vertical pull—
Into the stars—the stellar winds—she sails
High above the bones down below—the pieces
Crawling together where they fell—

This—she sings—dragging the old
Board and a new body back up to do it
Again—this—is why I love to die.

ART OF SEEING

Snake meets the child stumbling
Down the cold side of a small mountain
With razor scars on its wrists—
A small spray of purple lupines
In one hand—broken bird in the other.

The child stops crying
When it sees snake—asks—"when
There's nothing but silence why does
The bird awaken from slumber—
Why does anything awaken?"

Snake's not an answer machine—
He don't know anything and if he suspects
Something he forgets it so as
To remain in a state of bliss—

But the child won't look
Away—offers the flowers—offers
The bird—offers itself—

Snake says—"there is no world."
And the child brings both hands
Together—and makes one.

Chorus

The witness can't be trusted—she
Lives with angry voices twitching on her
Tongue like the tails of rats stuck
Head-first in a keg of beef—

Buried regrets heave up from shifting soil
In an attempt to join with the instincts
They ignored—a backhoe sorts through
The ruins of time where only the wind
Expects to touch anything of value—what
Is found is what is known—meaning little
Is found other than the acceptance
That comes with an impossible chore—

Trillions of creatures lived in one
Another only to die in each other
Too late to stop the murderous gratitude
That is the assemblage of desires
And greed called faith—what isn't complicit
Draws one breath and succumbs—even
Silence has days when it screams
Only of course no one can hear.

And the tedious cyclical violations—
The witness is foggy—but remembers—
The crusaders sleep in their heavy armor—
Dreaming of an ecclesiastical sunset
Above a swamp filled with sodden timber
To which lost gods cling for breath—dying
A little more each time believing ends—

The knights chopped the hands off captured
Saracens then stitched them to crude wooden
Crosses they flung into the enemy's camp
Just at daybreak when the sun glowed violet on the manes
Of horses drinking blood from the river—

The appearance of too much light
Starts a fire in the mind of camp followers
Huddled around the warmth of the
Current illness with their hearts on a stick—

The witness is not sure but all signs
Point to a moment when magic in the form
Of a gentle touch by gauntleted hands
Turned its back on the world in time
To survive in some other world
Where we find it again when we come.

It will be there in the first breath
Taken on the other side of this one—in
The moment appetite—the crude
Hunger for the dripping source
With its tangy herbal smell and bloodless
Window on forever and right now—
Turns into a phantom limb angels
Use to paint the afterlife the same
Chilled actinium of villagers
Running from a falling rose.

And the melisma of a suttee bride smokes
In the malachite bowl of the fallen church
Until the tears of the earth put that culture out—

The stick figure can't escape the drawing
Found inside an old chest in an attic where
An uncle committed suicide by re-reading the entries
He wrote in a journal from another war—

Nothing is true that can be named—
Thankfully—it is no longer necessary
To consider what is or isn't true—

In the time of considering the lie
Is born—even in the silence huckster
Ghouls are blowing horns and selling
Tickets to a boat ride through the fog—

The lie is the mirror where we measure
The breath not taken—or the unwillingness to
Breathe as the creatures disappear
Into a broken universe that will
Be gone once the fog clears—

We awaken here where we are
Or not at all—shifting between forms
As if nothing changes
But the condition of the roads
That lead back home—bent by

Desire for beauty and mercy—shaped
In the grasp of stockyard claws—twisted
Into amalgams of lust and dread—
Attendant to the confessions of
The body that brought us here—the cruel
Fingers—the lame hoofs—the bitten
Faces—the swallowed eyes—the grace
And dignity of impermanence
Carried through the fog to an empty

Beach where an opalescent shell
Rolls in the small waves—filled with
The blue songs of water—the origin
Stories of whales—murmur of kelp—of sun and moon
Entwined inside the whispering shell until
Something picks it up to listen—
And perhaps—if they act
In time—we are saved.

Language of Grief

I wrote the end of the poem—"Catching Waves"—at a time when my brother—Roger—was in a life and death struggle with cancer. He's my family—he's my friend. We've meant something to each other almost since birth and the trajectory of our lives has mostly been synchronous.

At the end of the first book in the Quartet—*Snake*—there's a poem, "Voices," written in an unknown language for my seventeen-year-old bulldog—Lila. She was dying and spent most of her last days curled on her pillow sleeping at my feet below the desk where I write.

That poem came out of a dream I don't remember with the exception of the odd vocalizations that were still in my mind when I woke up. I immediately wrote down the sounds—spelling them phonetically. The words made no sense to me—didn't say anything recognizable, but when I spoke the words there was a strange musical beauty to them. It took weeks before I saw the English poem hidden inside the apparently meaningless sounds.

It happened again in "Catching Waves." Only this time I knew to look for another poem inside the dream words—and found one. It's been pointed out to me there are other poems but this is the one I found. The words inside the words are both italicized and bolded.

There's something about opening your heart at the point in which a loved one is on the verge of death. Letting feelings come out unedited in sounds that resemble and perhaps are the true language of grief.

It's like a frogman hanging facedown over an abyss with no apparent bottom—gently bobbing in the current—boneless—sensing the presence of something down there—perhaps feeling beckoned. Gently called deeper into what waits.

Postscript—my brother, Roger, died September 17th, 2013. He never saw this poem. But I believe he's hearing it now.

NOTES

In the first book in the Quartet—*Snake*—planet Earth—in a retributive fury—removes all evidence of organic life from her body—it is during this catastrophic process that the collective entity—snake—appeared—

In the second book—*Second Wind*—the poems represent the voices wandering lost inside this entity—the fragments—the myths, histories, inklings, and whispers that ripple on after their source is gone—

In this—the third book in the Quartet—*The Hunger Sutras*—snake looks for the precipitative embedded in the flesh of disaster. She searches for an answer to the question—"must we eat one another to survive?"

In the silence of the unoccupied earth snake finds the ghost of hunger—the essential congress in which things live out of phase with grace—she dances with this ghost—listens to the earth—feels the urgency of old energy seeking new occupations—

The title poem—"Hunger Sutras"—is written loosely in iambic pentameter. That is to say there are ten syllables per line—a syllabic rather than metrical count. I don't know quite how this came to be so as always will defer to snake. But once into it I tried to honor the oral tradition—which subsequently allows—by changing the spoken rhythms—great latitude in the scansion of the lines. What appears to be an ictic or stressed syllable on the page may well be unstressed when spoken.

The Sutras are divided into sections. They come from no single witness but are the swirl songs of the gone funneled through time into a broken geography haunted by appetite—the unwritten page—

All of the poems in the Quartet come from the underlying fear of organisms knowing they are born to be eaten—that they will be scattered—infinitely fragmented—the narrative then is not linear but like a shattered mirror in which tiny pieces of the whole story are found—the sorting of these pieces back together into wholeness is both a personal and literary journey for the author.

In the Quartet snake's gender flickers between male and female. She is a composite entity—the collective lives in her—as it lives in all of us—and she speaks from both perspectives—often in the same poem. It was necessary to suspend presumptions about voice and gender and the weight of presumption both of them carry like a backpack filled with gold—that—no matter how valuable—must be—at some point—put down to go on.

The last two lines of the prologue to the title poem are snake honoring one of her teachers—the great William Carlos Williams.

BIOGRAPHICAL NOTE

The Hunger Sutras is the third book in the *Snake Quartet* by Gary Lemons. He has published six books of poetry—the last of which, *Snake: Second Wind* (Red Hen Press, 2016), is the second book of the *Snake Quartet*. For decades he fished Alaska, built grain elevators, worked high steel, and reforested the clear cuts of the Pacific Northwest. Currently he and his wife, the artist Nöle Giulini, teach yoga from their studio, Tenderpaws. Gary's next book, *Original Grace*, is the final book in the *Snake Quartet* and is scheduled to be published in 2020.